Lifesav
For Financial Freedom

by

Mack and Brenda Timberlake

Harrison House
Tulsa, Oklahoma

Lifesavers: For Financial Freedom
ISBN 0-89274-942-3
Copyright © 1996 by Mack and Brenda Timberlake
Christian Faith Center
101 S. Peachtree Street
P.O. Box 100
Creedmoor, North Carolina 27522

Published by Harrison House, Inc.
P.O. Box 35035
Tulsa, Oklahoma 74153

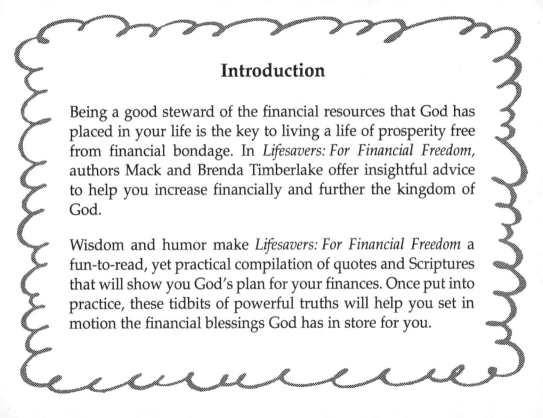

Introduction

Being a good steward of the financial resources that God has placed in your life is the key to living a life of prosperity free from financial bondage. In *Lifesavers: For Financial Freedom*, authors Mack and Brenda Timberlake offer insightful advice to help you increase financially and further the kingdom of God.

Wisdom and humor make *Lifesavers: For Financial Freedom* a fun-to-read, yet practical compilation of quotes and Scriptures that will show you God's plan for your finances. Once put into practice, these tidbits of powerful truths will help you set in motion the financial blessings God has in store for you.

**Decide that you will not
experience the curse of poverty,
but the blessings of prosperity.**

Christ hath redeemed us from the curse of the law, being made a curse for us: for it is written, Cursed is every one that hangeth on a tree:

That the blessing of Abraham might come on the Gentiles through Jesus Christ; that we might receive the promise of the Spirit through faith.
Galatians 3:13-14

The blessing of the Lord, it maketh rich,
and he addeth no sorrow with it.
Proverbs 10:22

God's pleasure increases
when His servants prosper.

Let them shout for joy, and be glad, that favour my
righteous cause: yea, let them say continually,
Let the Lord be magnified, which hath pleasure
in the prosperity of his servant.
Psalm 35:27

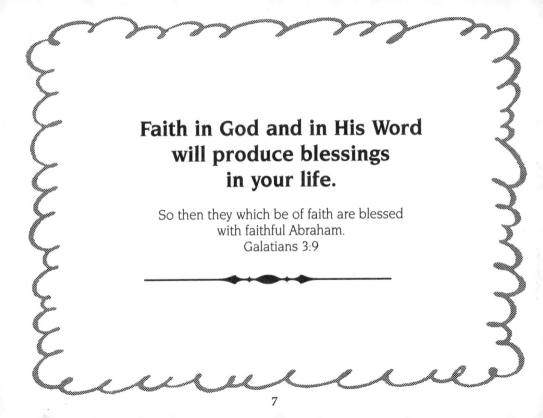

**Faith in God and in His Word
will produce blessings
in your life.**

So then they which be of faith are blessed
with faithful Abraham.
Galatians 3:9

**There is no shortage of provisions.
Get to know the Provider!**

The earth is the Lord's, and the fulness thereof;
the world, and they that dwell therein.
Psalm 24:1

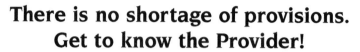

**See yourself rising above your
financial problems and accomplishing
victory with God's help.**

He hath raised us up together, and made us sit
together in heavenly places in Christ Jesus.
Ephesians 2:6

The "nature of reigning" is on the inside of every human.

And God said, Let us make man in our image, after our likeness: and let them have dominion over the fish of the sea, and over the fowl of the air, and over the cattle, and over all the earth, and over every creeping thing that creepeth upon the earth.
Genesis 1:26

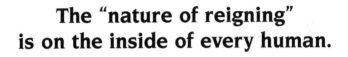

Think like a king and eventually you will achieve the lifestyle of a king.

And hast made us unto our God kings and priests:
and we shall reign on the earth.
Revelation 5:10

———◆◆◆———

Place wisdom at the top of your "things-to-get" list and watch good things come into your life.

For wisdom is better than rubies; and all the things
that may be desired are not to be compared to it.
Proverbs 8:11

Untapped resources are discovered by those whose joy and prayer life are maintained daily.

And when Jehoshaphat and his people came to take away the spoil of them, they found among them in abundance both riches with the dead bodies, and precious jewels, which they stripped off for themselves, more than they could carry away: and they were three days in gathering of the spoil, it was so much.
2 Chronicles 20:25

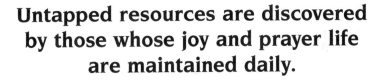

You will prosper when you help others to prosper.

And the Lord turned the captivity of Job,
when he prayed for his friends: also the Lord
gave Job twice as much as he had before.

Job 42:10

God is ready to give you more than what you are asking from Him.

And I have also given thee that which thou hast not asked,
both riches, and honour: so that there shall not be any
among the kings like unto thee all thy days.

1 Kings 3:13

The larger your heart becomes in giving, the larger your return will be.

He which soweth sparingly shall reap also sparingly; and he which soweth bountifully shall reap also bountifully.
2 Corinthians 9:6

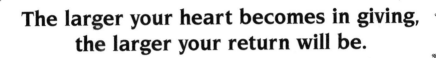

A desire for wisdom will draw financial favor into your life.

And she said to the king, It was a true report that I heard
in mine own land of thy acts and of thy wisdom.
Howbeit I believed not the words, until I came, and mine eyes
had seen it: and, behold, the half was not told me: thy wisdom
and prosperity exceedeth the fame which I heard.
And king Solomon gave unto the queen of Sheba all her desire, whatsoever she
asked, beside that which Solomon gave her of his royal bounty. . . .

1 Kings 10:6-7,13

God may not use traditional means to "heaven express" your resources to you.

And the ravens brought him bread and flesh in the morning,
and bread and flesh in the evening; and he drank of the brook.

1 Kings 17:6

There are unique gifts and talents in your life. Once perfected, they will yield continuous income.

And all the earth sought to Solomon, to hear his wisdom, which God had put in his heart.

And they brought every man his present, vessels of silver, and vessels of gold, and garments, and armour, and spices, horses, and mules, a rate year by year.
1 Kings 10:24-25

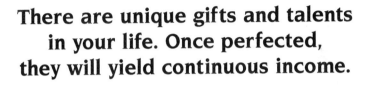

Willingness to give in obedience will draw your harvest to you.

For if there be first a willing mind, it is accepted according to that a man hath, and not according to that he hath not.

2 Corinthians 8:12

When you combine the power of the natural world (money) and the power of the spiritual world (the Holy Spirit), a righteous cause will be accomplished.

And the multitude of them that believed were of one heart and of one soul: neither said any of them that ought of the things which he possessed was his own; but they had all things common.

Acts 4:32

Riches and honor will amplify who you really are and what you really believe.

And the Lord was with Jehoshaphat, because he walked in the first ways of his father David, and sought not unto Baalim;

Therefore the Lord established the kingdom in his hand; and all Judah brought to Jehoshaphat presents; and he had riches and honour in abundance.
2 Chronicles 17:3,5

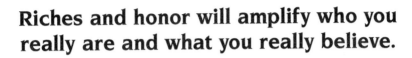

Your *vision* alone is not enough. God's *provision* is needed for your every vision.

And Abraham lifted up his eyes, and looked, and behold behind him a ram caught in a thicket by his horns: and Abraham went and took the ram, and offered him up for a burnt offering in the stead of his son.

Genesis 22:13

There are two sources that answer all things: God and money.

A feast is made for laughter, and wine maketh merry: but money answereth all things.

Ecclesiastes 10:19

There are many people who have riches and wealth and rejoice in their labor. You too can have this kind of joy.

Every man also to whom God hath given riches and wealth, and hath given him power to eat thereof, and to take his portion, and to rejoice in his labour; this is the gift of God.
Ecclesiastes 5:19

A good name is rather to be chosen than great riches,
and loving favour rather than silver and gold.
Proverbs 22:1

Salvation is more valuable than the riches of the world.

For what is a man profited, if he shall gain the
whole world, and lose his own soul? or what
shall a man give in exchange for his soul?
Matthew 16:26

Wisdom and understanding are more valuable than money.

Happy is the man that findeth wisdom, and the man that getteth understanding.

For the merchandise of it is better than the merchandise of silver, and the gain thereof than fine gold.
Proverbs 3:13-14

A godly wife is more valuable than money.

Who can find a virtuous woman? for her price is far above rubies.
Proverbs 31:10

Marriage is an economic covenant.

Imagine yourself actually enjoying your occupation with an increasing amount of income. These kind of imaginations are gifts from God waiting to be unwrapped.

Behold that which I have seen: it is good and comely for one to eat and to drink, and to enjoy the good of all his labour that he taketh under the sun all the days of his life, which God giveth him: for it is his portion.

Every man also to whom God hath given riches and wealth, and hath given him power to eat thereof, and to take his portion, and to rejoice in his labour; this is the gift of God.

Ecclesiastes 5:18-19

A higher income awaits those who don't become discouraged and give up.

And let us not be weary in well doing: for in due
season we shall reap, if we faint not.
Galatians 6:9

Dream, then drive for it.

Abraham knew the importance of the tithe before the law was written. Tithing was a vital key to his financial success.

And he [Melchizedek] blessed him, and said, Blessed be Abram of the most high God, possessor of heaven and earth:

And blessed be the most high God, which hath delivered thine enemies into thy hand. And he gave him tithes of all.
Genesis 14:19-20

Confidence in your face, handshake, and walk will aid you in getting a better job.

For the Lord shall be thy confidence,
and shall keep thy foot from being taken.
Proverbs 3:26

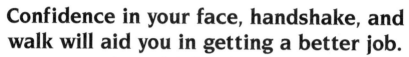

Diligence will propel you toward your financial goals.

The soul of the sluggard desireth, and hath nothing:
but the soul of the diligent shall be made fat.
Proverbs 13:4

When you seek God faithfully, you will be made a steward of what He owns.

But without faith it is impossible to please him: for he that cometh to God must believe that he is, and that he is a rewarder of them that diligently seek him.
Hebrews 11:6

Therefore I say unto you, What things soever ye desire, when ye pray, believe that ye receive them, and ye shall have them.
Mark 11:24

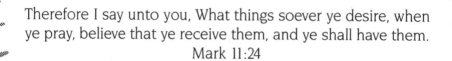

There is something in your life that has the potential of bringing you great promotion and recognition. Become an expert at what you do best.

Seest thou a man diligent in his business? he shall stand before kings; he shall not stand before mean men.
Proverbs 22:29

**When God is your partner
in business and in life,
promotion is inevitable.**

For promotion cometh neither from the east,
nor from the west, nor from the south.

But God is the judge: he putteth down one,
and setteth up another.
Psalm 75:6-7

A lack of supply in your present condition could be directly related to past conversations that were poverty-minded.

Teach me, and I will hold my tongue: and cause me to understand wherein I have erred.

Job 6:24

Death and life are in the power of the tongue: and they that love it shall eat the fruit thereof.

Proverbs 18:21

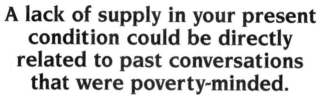

When God does not agree with us, heaven does not respond.

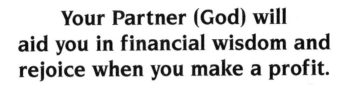

Your Partner (God) will aid you in financial wisdom and rejoice when you make a profit.

And Abram said to the king of Sodom, I have lift up mine hand unto the Lord, the most high God, the possessor of heaven and earth, That I will not take from a thread even to a shoelatchet, and that I will not take any thing that is thine, lest thou shouldest say, I have made Abram rich.
Genesis 14:22-23

And Abraham was old, and well stricken in age: and the Lord had blessed Abraham in all things.
Genesis 24:1

Kings are normally able to recognize God's hand upon a person's life. They readily invest in what God is doing through an individual.

And Abimelech took sheep, and oxen, and menservants, and womenservants, and gave them unto Abraham, and restored him Sarah his wife.
Genesis 20:14

God has already given you the power to get, create, invent, design, and procure wealth.

Riches and honour are with me [wisdom]; yea, durable riches and righteousness.
Proverbs 8:18

But thou shalt remember the Lord thy God: for it is he that giveth thee power to get wealth, that he may establish his covenant which he sware unto thy fathers, as it is this day.
Deuteronomy 8:18

When you possess something unique and attractive to the eye, people are willing to pay handsomely to obtain it.

And it came to pass, that, when Abram was come into Egypt, the Egyptians beheld the woman that she was very fair.
The princes also of Pharaoh saw her, and commended her before Pharaoh: and the woman was taken into Pharaoh's house.
And he entreated Abram well for her sake: and he had sheep, and oxen, and he asses, and menservants, and maidservants, and she asses, and camels.
Genesis 12:14-16

Givers never have a shortage of friends.

Many will intreat the favour of the prince: and every
man is a friend to him that giveth gifts.
Proverbs 19:6

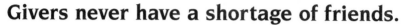

Become a bridge builder by
secretly giving a gift to someone
who needs a smile.

A gift in secret pacifieth anger: and a
reward in the bosom strong wrath.
Proverbs 21:14

**Your abilities and talents,
once perfected and tested, have the
potential to bring you instant promotion.**

And Pharaoh said unto his servants, Can we find such a one as this is, a man in whom the Spirit of God is?

And Pharaoh said unto Joseph, Forasmuch as God hath shewed thee all this, there is none so discreet and wise as thou art:

Thou shalt be over my house, and according unto thy word shall all my people be ruled: only in the throne will I be greater than thou.
Genesis 41:38-40

**A gift communicates to others
that they were on your mind.**

A gift is as a precious stone in the eyes of him
that hath it: whithersoever it turneth, it prospereth.
Proverbs 17:8

**You are only one creative idea away
from becoming a millionaire.**

Worship and giving are kindred spirits that inspire God to move on your behalf.

Three times in a year shall all thy males appear before the Lord thy God in the place which he shall choose; in the feast of unleavened bread, and in the feast of weeks, and in the feast of tabernacles: and they shall not appear before the Lord empty:

Every man shall give as he is able, according to the blessing of the Lord thy God which he hath given thee.
Deuteronomy 16:16-17

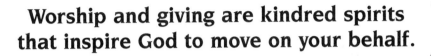

How you think about money reveals how you think about life.

For as he thinketh in his heart, so is he. . . .
Proverbs 23:7a

Your life and your finances will never be the same again when you find a need and fill it.

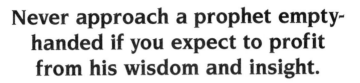

Never approach a prophet empty-handed if you expect to profit from his wisdom and insight.

And he said unto him, Behold now, there is in this city a man of God, and he is an honourable man; all that he saith cometh surely to pass: now let us go thither; peradventure he can shew us our way that we should go.

Then said Saul to his servant, But, behold, if we go, what shall we bring the man? for the bread is spent in our vessels, and there is not a present to bring to the man of God: what have we?

And the servant answered Saul again, and said, Behold, I have here at hand the fourth part of a shekel of silver: that will I give to the man of God, to tell us our way.

1 Samuel 9:6-8

Accountability is an invitation for increase.

He that is faithful in that which is least is faithful also in much: and he that is unjust in the least is unjust also in much.

Luke 16:10

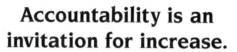

Find some way to generate income beyond your "8-to-5" job.

I wisdom dwell with prudence, and find out knowledge of witty inventions.

Proverbs 8:12

With money we bargain, trade, and exchange our way through life.

Then she came and told the man of God.
And he said, Go, sell the oil, and pay thy debt,
and live thou and thy children of the rest.

2 Kings 4:7

Learn how to make money and it will serve you well.

And I say unto you, Make to yourselves friends
of the mammon of unrighteousness; that, when ye fail,
they may receive you into everlasting habitations.

Luke 16:9

One kind act of hospitality can multiply into a miracle that will last a lifetime.

And it fell on a day, that Elisha passed to Shunem, where was a great woman; and she constrained him to eat bread. And so it was, that as oft as he passed by, he turned in thither to eat bread.

And he said to Gehazi his servant, Call this Shunammite. And when he had called her, she stood before him.

And he said unto him, Say now unto her, Behold, thou hast been careful for us with all this care; what is to be done for thee? wouldest thou be spoken for to the king, or to the captain of the host? And she answered, I dwell among mine own people.

And he said, What then is to be done for her? And Gehazi answered, Verily she hath no child, and her husband is old.

And he said, Call her. And when he had called her, she stood in the door.

And he said, About this season, according to the time of life, thou shalt embrace a son. And she said, Nay, my lord, thou man of God, do not lie unto thine handmaid.

And the woman conceived, and bare a son at that season that Elisha had said unto her, according to the time of life.
2 Kings 4:8-17

Find a ministry that heals
and invest in it generously.

Now Naaman, captain of the host of the king of Syria, was a great man with his master, and honourable, because by him the Lord had given deliverance unto Syria: he was also a mighty man in valour, but he was a leper.

And the Syrians had gone out by companies, and had brought away captive out of the land of Israel a little maid; and she waited on Naaman's wife.

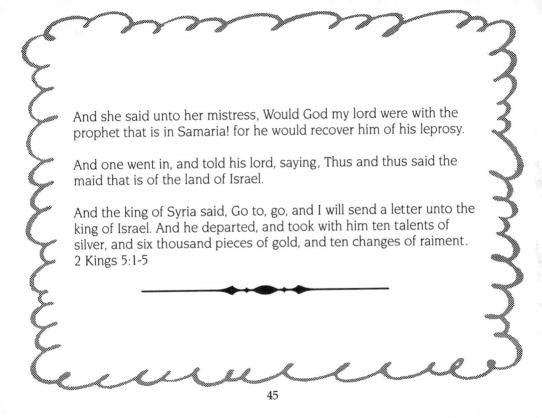

And she said unto her mistress, Would God my lord were with the prophet that is in Samaria! for he would recover him of his leprosy.

And one went in, and told his lord, saying, Thus and thus said the maid that is of the land of Israel.

And the king of Syria said, Go to, go, and I will send a letter unto the king of Israel. And he departed, and took with him ten talents of silver, and six thousand pieces of gold, and ten changes of raiment. 2 Kings 5:1-5

**Share the fruits of your success
with those who have helped you
succeed and with those whose help
you will need in the future.**

And when David came to Ziklag, he sent of the spoil unto
the elders of Judah, even to his friends, saying, Behold a
present for you of the spoil of the enemies of the Lord.
1 Samuel 30:26

Double honor equals double wages.

Let the elders that rule well be counted worthy
of double honour, especially they who labour
in the word and doctrine.
1 Timothy 5:17

Debt is when you owe something and don't have the money to pay it.

It is wise not to withhold money.

Withhold not good from them to whom it is due,
when it is in the power of thine hand to do it.
Proverbs 3:27

Allow God — your Divine Connection — to usher in your divine prosperity.

And Elisha came to Damascus; and Ben-hadad the king of Syria was sick; and it was told him, saying, The man of God is come hither.

And the king said unto Hazael, Take a present in thine hand, and go, meet the man of God, and enquire of the Lord by him, saying, Shall I recover of this disease?
2 Kings 8:7-8

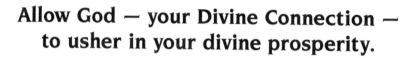

Develop your faith in God's ability to supply your needs.

Now unto him that is able to do exceeding abundantly above all that we ask or think, according to the power that worketh in us.

Ephesians 3:20

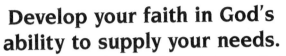

Never covet another's wealth. Remember, there is an abundance of wealth unclaimed.

Finances will come your way when you provide excellent service.

And it came to pass afterward, that he went throughout every city and village, preaching and shewing the glad tidings of the kingdom of God: and the twelve were with him,

And certain women, which had been healed of evil spirits and infirmities, Mary called Magdalene, out of whom went seven devils,

And Joanna the wife of Chuza Herod's steward, and Susanna, and many others, which ministered unto him of their substance.
Luke 8:1-3

People who commit their goals to paper will soon write their own checks.

And the Lord answered me, and said, Write the vision, and make it plain upon tables, that he may run that readeth it.
Habakkuk 2:2

Money flows towards good ideas.

Abundance comes from the Almighty.

If thou return to the Almighty, thou shalt be built up, thou shalt put away iniquity far from thy tabernacles.

Then shalt thou lay up gold as dust, and the gold of Ophir as the stones of the brooks.

Yea, the Almighty shall be thy defense, and thou shalt have plenty of silver.
Job 22:23-25

Set an attainable goal for your financial future.

Commit thy works unto the Lord, and thy
thoughts shall be established.
Proverbs 16:3

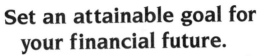

Lack of financial goals will keep your head and your life in a constant spending mode.

Your giving is a reflection of your faith in God.

And he called unto him his disciples, and saith unto them, Verily I say unto you, That this poor widow hath cast more in, than all they which have cast into the treasury:

For all they did cast in of their abundance; but she of her want did cast in all that she had, even all her living.
Mark 12:43-44

**Spending more than you can afford
is an indicator that you are not
enjoying the life you are living.**

**Choose a mentor who has already
achieved your desired financial goal
and learn from him or her.**

The queen of the south shall rise up in the judgment with
this generation, and shall condemn it: for she came from the
uttermost parts of the earth to hear the wisdom of
Solomon; and, behold, a greater than Solomon is here.
Matthew 12:42

What you do for God's house,
He will do for your house.

Now when he had ended all his sayings in the audience of the people, he entered into Capernaum.

And a certain centurion's servant, who was dear unto him, was sick, and ready to die.

And when he heard of Jesus, he sent unto him the elders of the Jews, beseeching him that he would come and heal his servant.

And when they came to Jesus, they besought him instantly, saying, That he was worthy for whom he should do this:

For he loveth our nation, and he hath built us a synagogue.

Wherefore neither thought I myself [the centurion] worthy to come unto thee: but say in a word, and my servant shall be healed.

And they that were sent, returning to the house, found the servant whole that had been sick.
Luke 7:1-5,7,10

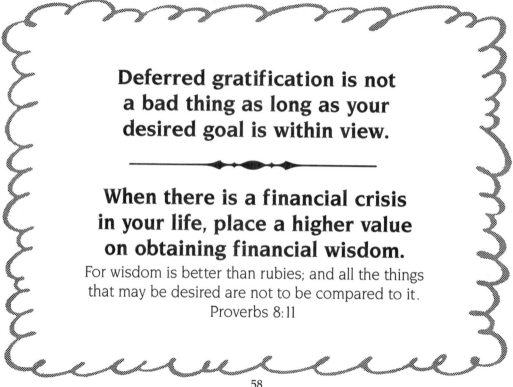

**Deferred gratification is not
a bad thing as long as your
desired goal is within view.**

**When there is a financial crisis
in your life, place a higher value
on obtaining financial wisdom.**

For wisdom is better than rubies; and all the things
that may be desired are not to be compared to it.
Proverbs 8:11

Money identifies with the character of the beholder.

But they that will be rich fall into temptation and a snare, and into many foolish and hurtful lusts, which drown men in destruction and perdition.

For the love of money is the root of all evil: which while some coveted after, they have erred from the faith, and pierced themselves through with many sorrows.
1 Timothy 6:9-10

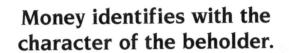

The cheapest car to drive is probably the one you are driving especially when you compare the repair bill to the cost of purchasing a new car.

Don't become angry at the rich. Instead, become a student and learn from them.

Hear instruction, and be wise, and refuse it not.
Proverbs 8:33

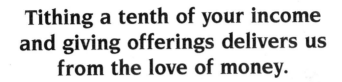

Tithing a tenth of your income and giving offerings delivers us from the love of money.

Charge them that are rich in this world, that they be not high-minded, nor trust in uncertain riches, but in the living God, who giveth us richly all things to enjoy;

That they do good, that they be rich in good works, ready to distribute, willing to communicate;

Laying up in store for themselves a good foundation against the time to come, that they may lay hold on eternal life.
1 Timothy 6:17-19

61

**The three wise men knew the
power of giving to the true King.
Join the number of people who are wise.**

And when they were come into the house,
they saw the young child with Mary his mother,
and fell down, and worshiped him: and when
they had opened their treasures, they presented
unto him gifts; gold, and frankincense, and myrrh.

Matthew 2:11

**Prepare to make the rules
when you own the gold.**

So king Solomon exceeded all the kings
of the earth for riches and for wisdom.

1 Kings 10:23

There can be a down-side to money if your heart is not in right standing with God.

Then one of the twelve, called Judas Iscariot, went unto the chief priests,

And said unto them, What will ye give me, and I will deliver him unto you? And they covenanted with him for thirty pieces of silver.

And from that time he sought opportunity to betray him.
Matthew 26:14-16

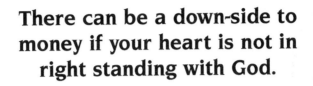

Riches come in degrees.

And these are they which are sown on good ground; such as hear the word, and receive it, and bring forth fruit, some thirtyfold, some sixty, and some an hundred.

Mark 4:20

Arrange your finances so that taxes are as low as possible.

Labour not to be rich: cease from thine own wisdom.

Proverbs 23:3

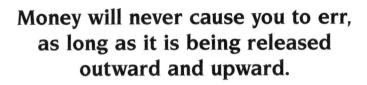

Money will never cause you to err, as long as it is being released outward and upward.

It is easier for a camel to go through the eye of a needle, than for a rich man to enter into the kingdom of God.

And they were astonished out of measure, saying among themselves, Who then can be saved?

And Jesus looking upon them saith, With men it is impossible, but not with God: for with God all things are possible.
Mark 10:25-27

Allow *anticipation* to motivate your *participation* in the progress of your future.

The love of God and the blessings of God are two different things. God loves you unconditionally, but His blessings are conditional upon your obedience to His Word.

If ye be willing and obedient,
ye shall eat the good of the land.
Isaiah 1:19

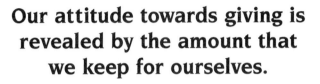

Our attitude towards giving is revealed by the amount that we keep for ourselves.

And he called unto him his disciples, and saith unto them, Verily I say unto you, That this poor widow hath cast more in, than all they which have cast into the treasury:

For all they did cast in of their abundance; but she of her want did cast in all that she had, even all her living.
Mark 12:43-44

Never make financial decisions under pressure or when you are in a hurry.

Be willing to discipline yourself immediately for long-term gain.

When God owns your life and your money you will experience His best.

Then Jesus beholding him loved him, and said unto him, One thing thou lackest: go thy way, sell whatsoever thou hast, and give to the poor, and thou shalt have treasure in heaven: and come, take up the cross, and follow me.

And he was sad at that saying, and went away grieved: for he had great possessions.
Mark 10:21-22

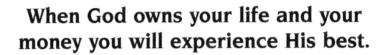

Allow heaven's riches to become an earthly reality by giving to a heavenly cause.

But my God shall supply all your need according to his riches in glory by Christ Jesus.
Philippians 4:19

The man who is under Christian instruction should be willing to compensate his teacher and counselor.

Let him that is taught in the word communicate unto him that teacheth in all good things.
Galatians 6:6

The good news to the poor is that they no longer have to be poor. There is so much abundance to go around.

The Spirit of the Lord is upon me, because he hath anointed me to preach the gospel to the poor; he hath sent me to heal the brokenhearted, to preach deliverance to the captives, and recovering of sight to the blind, to set at liberty them that are bruised,

To preach the acceptable year of the Lord.
Luke 4:18-19

Find something, such as vending machines or rental properties, that will generate income for you in your absence.

Set a goal to obtain income on a daily basis rather than a salary on a weekly or monthly basis.

Blessed be the Lord, who daily loadeth us with benefits, even the God of our salvation. Selah.
Psalm 68:19

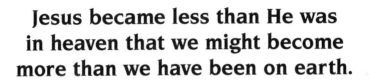

Jesus became less than He was in heaven that we might become more than we have been on earth.

Let this mind be in you, which was also in Christ Jesus:
Who, being in the form of God, thought it not robbery
to be equal with God:
But made himself of no reputation, and took upon him
the form of a servant, and was made in the likeness of men:
And being found in fashion as a man, he humbled himself,
and became obedient unto death, even the death of the cross.
Philippians 2:5-8

. . .I am come that they might have life, and that they might have it more
abundantly.
John 10:10

**Out of every 100 people
at the age of 65. . .**

a) 36% are dead
b) 4% are well to do
c) 5% are still working
d) 54% are totally dependent on others
e) 1% are wealthy

(Source: U.S. Department of Health and Human Services—Insurance
Industry Statistics)

Of the 1% who are wealthy at age 65. . .

a) 5% were salesmen

b) 10% were CEOs and presidents of corporations

c) 10% were doctors and lawyers

d) 1% were athletes, entertainers, or lottery winners

e) 74% were people who owned their own businesses

(Source: U.S. Department of Health and Human Services—Insurance Industry Statistics)

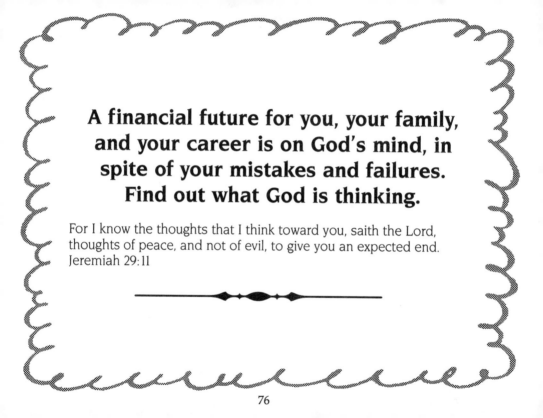

A financial future for you, your family, and your career is on God's mind, in spite of your mistakes and failures. Find out what God is thinking.

For I know the thoughts that I think toward you, saith the Lord, thoughts of peace, and not of evil, to give you an expected end. Jeremiah 29:11

**Spend less than you make
for a long time and you will have
money for as long as you live.**

**Three important factors that
determine financial prosperity:
a) what you spend,
b) what you sow or share, and
c) what you save.**

God is reward-conscious so it makes good sense to become a co-laborer with Him.

But without faith it is impossible to please him: for he that cometh to God must believe that he is, and that he is a rewarder of them that diligently seek him.
Hebrews 11:6

Never allow your imagination to dwell on any episode of failure. Dream again for there is a brighter ending for those who never give up.

And let us not be weary in well doing: for in due season we shall reap, if we faint not.
Galatians 6:9

Small thinkers always get minimum wages.

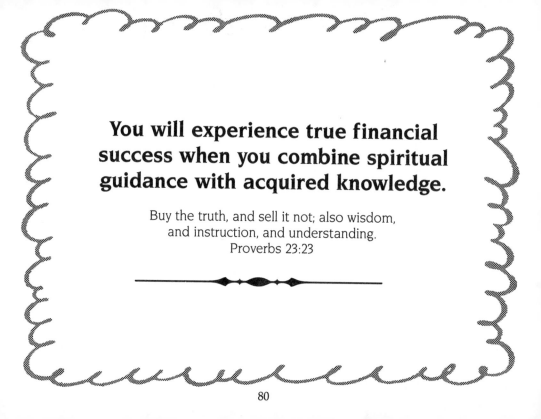

You will experience true financial success when you combine spiritual guidance with acquired knowledge.

Buy the truth, and sell it not; also wisdom,
and instruction, and understanding.
Proverbs 23:23

**God's interest in real estate proved
to be a profit of vast multiplication.
Experience what Adam felt in the
Garden of Eden when God placed
him in prime real estate.**

And the Lord God took the man, and put him
into the garden of Eden to dress it and to keep it.
Genesis 2:15

**Trust in God for your rewards
such as wages, compensation,
and salary by tithing.**

**A suggested budget that promotes
a solid financial future:**

a) 10% to God,
b) 70% for living expenses,
c) 10% for emergencies and
savings, and
d) 10% for investments for the future.

You are in debt if the current value of a
purchase is less than what you owe on it.

People with the goal of being
debt-free soon discover the necessity
of deciding what they must have,
should have, and would like to have.

**If you are an impulsive buyer,
return the items that you
purchased yesterday and today.**

He that loveth pleasure shall be a poor man: he that loveth wine and
oil shall not be rich.
Proverbs 21:17

The words "paid in full"
never bring sorrow and regret
but happiness and relief.

If you are in a financial pinch,
correct what is causing the pain.

If you expect to get rich quick, you are already standing on shaky ground.

A faithful man shall abound with blessings: but he that maketh haste to be rich shall not be innocent.
Proverbs 28:20

Never say that God is testing your faith
when you have frustrated His grace.

———◆———

Don't become an easy prey to financial
disaster by your inability to say "no" to a
sales pitch. Say "No, thank you" twice
as much as "How much?"

As heirs of God, the blessings God gave to Abraham are available to us.

And Abram was very rich in cattle, in silver, and in gold.
Genesis 13:2

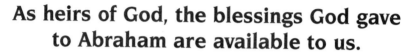

And if ye be Christ's, then are ye Abraham's seed,
and heirs according to the promise.
Galatians 3:29

If accumulation of wealth is your ambition there will be little time for the valuable things in life.

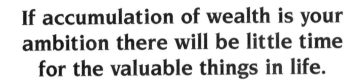

Financially speaking, God always blesses everyone who acts upon His principles.

Then Peter opened his mouth, and said, Of a truth
I perceive that God is no respecter of persons.
Acts 10:34

God is in search of partners who want guaranteed financial prosperity.

Praise ye the Lord. Blessed is the man that feareth the Lord, that delighteth greatly in his commandments.

His seed shall be mighty upon earth: the generation of the upright shall be blessed.

Wealth and riches shall be in his house: and his righteousness endureth for ever.
Psalm 112:1-3

For the Lord God is a sun and shield:
the Lord will give grace and glory: no good thing
will he withhold from them that walk uprightly.
Psalms 84:11

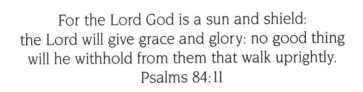

Decide to be excellent in all you do and you will attract people with great riches into your life.

When the even was come, there came a
rich man of Arimathaea, named Joseph,
who also himself was Jesus' disciple.
Matthew 27:57

You have lost sight of God's richness when you are looking at what is in His hand, instead of looking at His face.

And he sought God in the days of Zechariah, who had understanding in the visions of God: and as long as he sought the Lord, God made him to prosper.
2 Chronicles 26:5

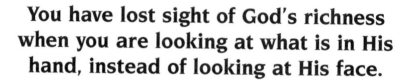

There is an abundance of wealth and wisdom in God's law of prosperity.

If money, success, recognition, possessions, and a better job are at the top of your prayer requests, it is time to realign your priorities.

By humility and the fear of the Lord
are riches, and honour, and life.
Proverbs 22:4

**You have located the source
of riches and honor when God
is at the center of your life.**

I love them that love me [wisdom]; and those that seek
me early shall find me.

Riches and honour are with me; yea,
durable riches and righteousness.
Proverbs 8:17-18

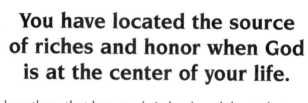

**Freedom from financial problems is one
of the benefits of God's perfect peace.**

Thou wilt keep him in perfect peace, whose mind is stayed
on thee: because he trusteth in thee.
Isaiah 26:3

**Emptiness is always the result of
a "buy now, pay later" lifestyle.**

If you think with your head and not with your heart, money will become your god.

For the love of money is the root of all evil: which while some coveted after, they have erred from the faith, and pierced themselves through with many sorrows.
1 Timothy 6:10

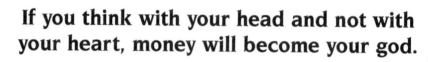

Thus saith the Lord, thy Redeemer, the Holy One of Israel; I am the Lord thy God which teacheth thee to profit, which leadeth thee by the way that thou shouldest go.
Isaiah 48:17

Going the extra mile on your job will produce extra pay.

And whatsoever ye do, do it heartily, as to the Lord, and not unto men.
Colossians 3:23

In the midst of an economic crisis, God will show you how to prosper.

And there was a famine in the land, beside the first famine that was in the days of Abraham. And Isaac went unto Abimelech king of the Philistines unto Gerar.

Then Isaac sowed in that land, and received in the same year an hundredfold: and the Lord blessed him.
Genesis 26:1,12

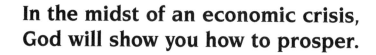

Your attitude about giving will determine what God will return to you.

Every man according as he purposeth
in his heart, so let him give; not grudgingly,
or of necessity: for God loveth a cheerful giver.
2 Corinthians 9:7

Experience the security of a job with promotions and raises when you increase the worth of your employer.

Whatsoever thy hand findeth to do, do it with thy might;
for there is no work, nor device, nor knowledge,
nor wisdom, in the grave, whither thou goest.
Ecclesiastes 9:10

Financial breakthroughs are usually discovered after you conquer the fear of risk.

He shall not be afraid of evil tidings: his heart is fixed, trusting in the Lord.

His heart is established, he shall not be afraid, until he see his desire upon his enemies.
Psalm 112:7-8

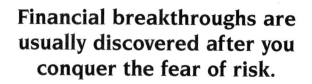

**Your mind is like a computer.
Programming determines output.**

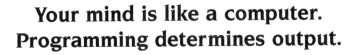

**Become the captain of your ship
and sail for the harbor that
contains peace and prosperity.**

And the Lord shall guide thee continually, and satisfy
thy soul in drought, and make fat thy bones: and thou
shalt be like a watered garden, and like a spring
of water, whose waters fail not.
Isaiah 58:11

For successful living,
direct your giving . . .

a) First toward God,
Honour the Lord with thy substance, and with the firstfruits of all thine increase:
Proverbs 3:9

b) To your family,
But if any provide not for his own, and specially for those of his own house, he hath denied the faith, and is worse than an infidel.
1 Timothy 5:8

c) To other Christians, and
As we have therefore opportunity, let us do good unto all men, especially unto them who are of the household of faith.
Galatians 6:10

d) To the poor.
He that hath pity upon the poor lendeth unto the Lord; and that which he hath given will he pay him again.
Proverbs 19:17

When you incur debt a large portion of your money goes for interest and a carrying charge. You pay more and get less.

He that oppresseth the poor to increase his riches, and he that giveth to the rich, shall surely come to want.

Proverbs 22:16

Perform a task well and then find ways of marketing what you do.

**Building wealth is like climbing stairs.
You are not likely to stumble if you
take one step at a time.**

For the earth bringeth forth fruit of herself; first the blade, then the
ear, after that the full corn in the ear.

But when the fruit is brought forth, immediately he putteth in the
sickle, because the harvest is come.
Mark 4:28-29

If you don't know what you
are doing, you are making someone
else, who thrives off your ignorance,
increasingly rich.

Become a financial specialist with the
ability to analyze your situation, and
decide a workable solution.

You are successful when your increased earnings are void of increased pressure.

And these are they which are sown among thorns; such as hear the word,

And the cares of this world, and the deceitfulness of riches, and the lusts of other things entering in, choke the word, and it becometh unfruitful.
Mark 4:18-19

The best paid people are those who perform best under pressure.

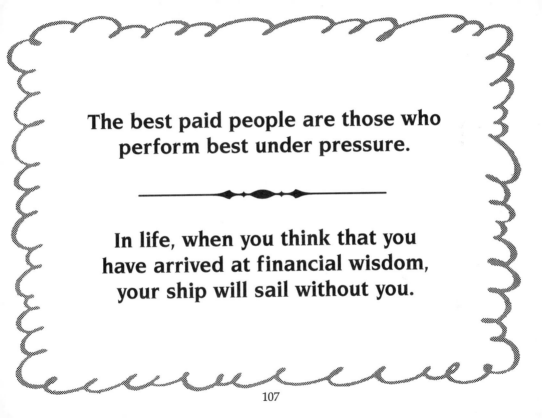

In life, when you think that you have arrived at financial wisdom, your ship will sail without you.

If you are able to work effectively without supervision, you are destined to be a supervisor over money.

Go to the ant, thou sluggard; consider her ways, and be wise:

Which having no guide, overseer, or ruler,

Provideth her meat in the summer, and gathereth her food in the harvest.
Proverbs 6:6-8

When pressure comes, guard your mind. Don't allow pressure to change a positive attitude into a negative one.

———◆———

Never spend more time listening to a critic than to the inward voice of God.

Give expecting to receive.

Give, and it shall be given unto you; good measure, pressed down, and shaken together, and running over, shall men give into your bosom. For with the same measure that ye mete withal it shall be measured to you again.
Luke 6:38

If you don't love what you are doing, get out and find something you do love before you are fired or go bankrupt.

If you supply what people need and want, people will confirm to you that there is no shortage of money.

When financial pressure comes against your life, tithe your way out of that pressure. Never let it stop you from giving.

He that observeth the wind shall not sow; and he that regardeth the clouds shall not reap.

In the morning sow thy seed, and in the evening withhold not thine hand: for thou knowest not whether shall prosper, either this or that, or whether they both shall be alike good.
Ecclesiastes 11:4,6

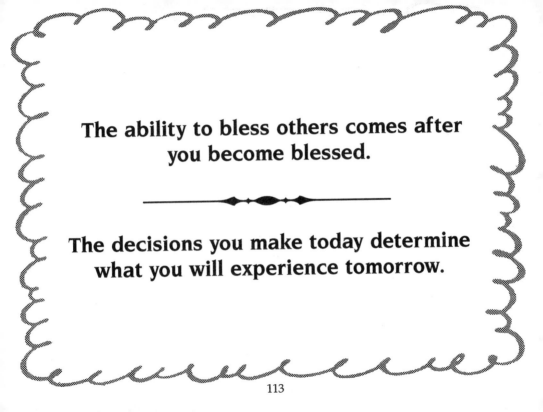

The ability to bless others comes after you become blessed.

The decisions you make today determine what you will experience tomorrow.

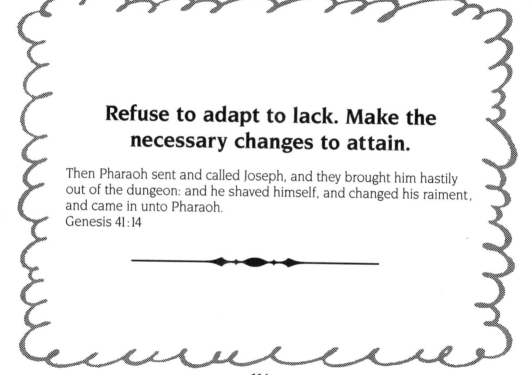

Refuse to adapt to lack. Make the necessary changes to attain.

Then Pharaoh sent and called Joseph, and they brought him hastily out of the dungeon: and he shaved himself, and changed his raiment, and came in unto Pharaoh.
Genesis 41:14

You are worth more than your paycheck.
Don't settle for anything less.

People who get along with others
are of great value. It is a learned
skill that produces great results.

God gives us His ability to obtain wealth in order to help others find Him.

But thou shalt remember the Lord thy God: for it is he that giveth thee power to get wealth, that he may establish his covenant which he sware unto thy fathers, as it is this day.
Deuteronomy 8:18

There is that maketh himself rich, yet hath nothing: there is that maketh himself poor, yet hath great riches.
Proverbs 13:7

Money management means knowing the difference between wasting money, hoarding money, spending money, and giving money.

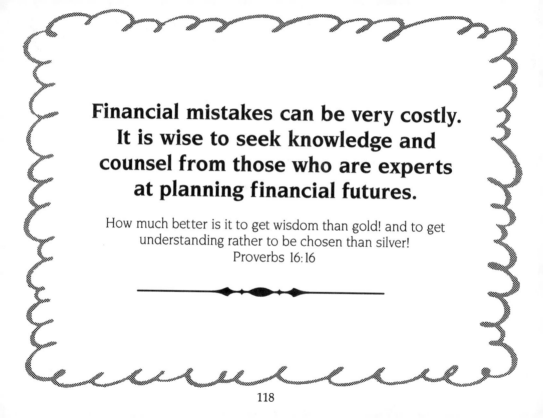

**Financial mistakes can be very costly.
It is wise to seek knowledge and
counsel from those who are experts
at planning financial futures.**

How much better is it to get wisdom than gold! and to get
understanding rather to be chosen than silver!
Proverbs 16:16

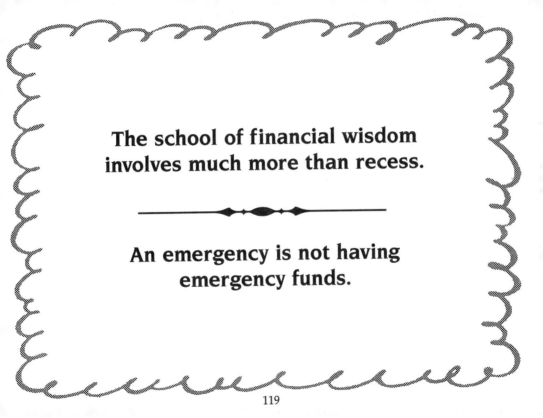

The school of financial wisdom involves much more than recess.

An emergency is not having emergency funds.

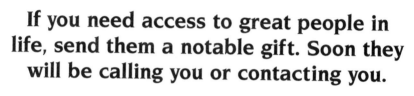

If you need access to great people in life, send them a notable gift. Soon they will be calling you or contacting you.

A man's gift maketh room for him,
and bringeth him before great men.
Proverbs 18:16

Ignoring taxes will give you a life
sustained by tax payers.

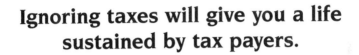

The cycle of poverty and debt engulfs
those who continually travel the
path of ignorance, indulgence,
and poor planning.

The first month you find yourself unable to pay the total charges on your credit cards, perform plastic surgery on your cards. It's the least expensive surgery.

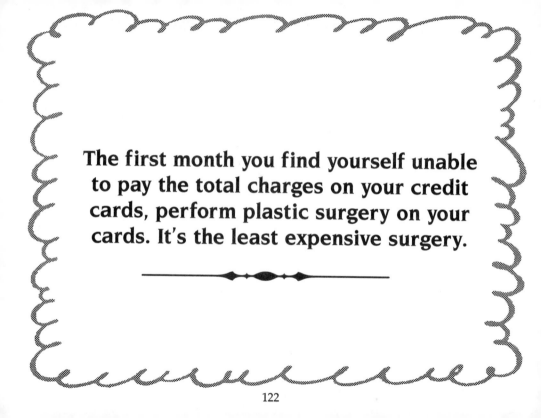

If you buy things to make yourself feel better, don't get sick often.

Living in a house that is too expensive for your budget will cause a domestic explosion.

Your financial prosperity is connected to past giving to God's servants and your obedience to the Word.

Let them shout for joy, and be glad, that favour my righteous cause: yea, let them say continually, Let the Lord be magnified, which hath pleasure in the prosperity of his servant.
Psalm 35:27

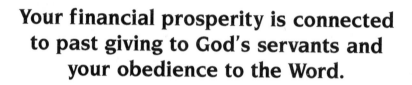

Don't allow a mortgage to give you a morgue temperament. Make extra payments on the principle for a resurrected feeling.

<hr>

If you get laid off or fired, don't get angry, get creative and become the president of your own company.

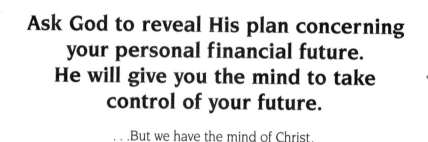

Ask God to reveal His plan concerning your personal financial future. He will give you the mind to take control of your future.

. . .But we have the mind of Christ.
1 Corinthians 2:16b

Those who remain in poverty seldom realize they are where they are as the result of their own habits.

If you find a path with no obstacles, there will be no gold at the end of your journey.

**When you desire to bless the poor
God will desire to bless you.**

He that hath pity upon the poor lendeth unto the Lord;
and that which he hath given will he pay him again.
Proverbs 19:17

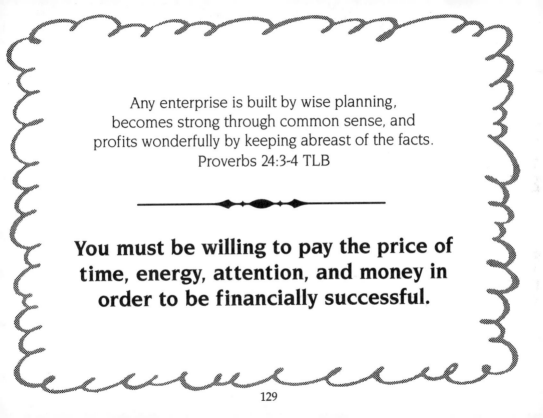

Any enterprise is built by wise planning,
becomes strong through common sense, and
profits wonderfully by keeping abreast of the facts.
Proverbs 24:3-4 TLB

**You must be willing to pay the price of
time, energy, attention, and money in
order to be financially successful.**

Purpose to be so good at what you do now that in the future your family and friends will reap favor just by the mention of your name.

And Pharaoh said unto Joseph, Say unto thy brethren, This do ye; lade your beasts, and go, get you unto the land of Canaan;

And take your father and your households, and come unto me: and I will give you the good of the land of Egypt, and ye shall eat the fat of the land.
Genesis 45:17-18

Learn from your past but don't live there.

For a just man falleth seven times, and riseth up again: but the wicked shall fall into mischief.
Proverbs 24:16

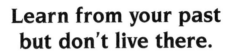

God made you to fly, not to fall, to climb, not to fall, to soar not to sink.

God's ways of gaining money:

a) by working
In all labour there is profit. . . .
Proverbs 14:23

b) by saving and investing
There is treasure to be desired and oil in the dwelling of the wise; but a foolish man spendeth it up.
Proverbs 21:20

c) by planning
Be thou diligent to know the state of thy flocks, and look well to thy herds. For riches are not for ever. . . .
Proverbs 27:23-24

When financial arrangements are made
easy, rates are usually higher.

When making a purchase, be sure
that your warranty covers things
that normally wear out.

When you feel that your boss is unfair, remember the following lifesavers:

a) But he that doeth wrong shall receive for the wrong which he hath done: and there is no respect of persons.
Colossians 3:25

b) Do all things without murmuring and disputings.
Philippians 2:14

c) See that none render evil for evil unto any man; but ever follow that which is good. . . .
1 Thessalonians 5:15

The longer the loan, the more interest you will pay. This means you will soon lose interest in what you were interested in purchasing.

It is better to give than to receive.

I have shewed you all things, how that so labouring
ye ought to support the weak, and to remember
the words of the Lord Jesus, how he said,
It is more blessed to give than to receive.
Acts 20:35

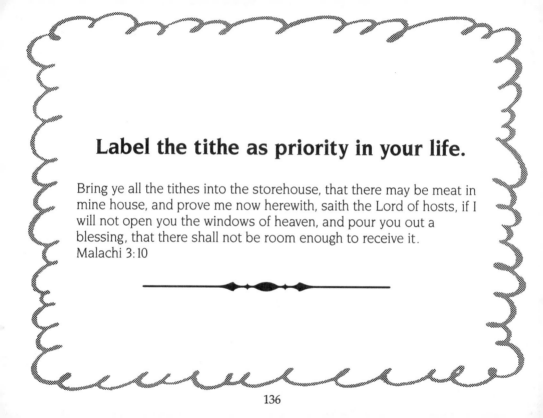

Label the tithe as priority in your life.

Bring ye all the tithes into the storehouse, that there may be meat in mine house, and prove me now herewith, saith the Lord of hosts, if I will not open you the windows of heaven, and pour you out a blessing, that there shall not be room enough to receive it.
Malachi 3:10

You only steal from yourself when you fail to manage your money.

Wanted! Good personnel who can manage silver and gold.

The silver is mine, and the gold is mine,
saith the Lord of hosts.
Haggai 2:8

Men and women under Christian instruction should be willing to contribute toward the livelihood of the Teacher.

Let him that is taught in the word communicate unto him that teacheth in all good things.
Galatians 6:6

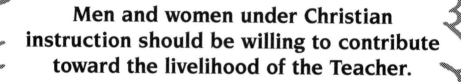

There are lots of uses for credit cards.
Think again before using one.

Spending less than what you make
always makes good cents.

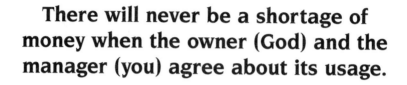

There will never be a shortage of money when the owner (God) and the manager (you) agree about its usage.

Thine, O Lord, is the greatness, and the power, and the glory, and the victory, and the majesty: for all that is in the heaven and in the earth is thine; thine is the kingdom, O Lord, and thou art exalted as head above all.

Both riches and honour come of thee, and thou reignest over all; and in thine hand is power and might; and in thine hand it is to make great, and to give strength unto all.

1 Chronicles 29:11-12

Deposits into your heavenly account can only be made from an earthly position.

Laying up in store for themselves a good foundation against the time to come, that they may lay hold on eternal life.
1 Timothy 6:19

Opportunities are always available for development, regardless of the state of the economy.

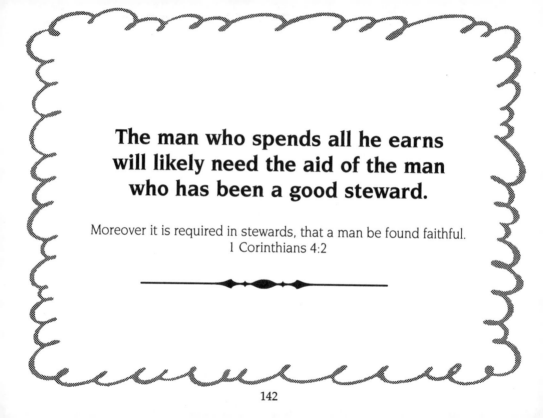

**The man who spends all he earns
will likely need the aid of the man
who has been a good steward.**

Moreover it is required in stewards, that a man be found faithful.
1 Corinthians 4:2

The truth about our spending habits will be revealed in the heavenly court.

For we must all appear before the judgment seat of Christ; that every one may receive the things done in his body, according to that he hath done, whether it be good or bad.

2 Corinthians 5:10

Weeping will endure longer than a night if you have no savings.

**True peace comes when we
conduct the affairs of our life
according to God's expectations.**

His lord said unto him, Well done, thou good and faithful servant:
thou hast been faithful over a few things, I will make thee ruler over
many things: enter thou into the joy of thy lord.
Matthew 25:21

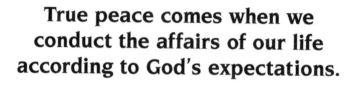

The resources come from one source.

And he said, I am Abraham's servant.
And the Lord hath blessed my master greatly;
and he is become great: and he hath given him flocks,
and herds, and silver, and gold, and menservants,
and maidservants, and camels, and asses.
Genesis 24:34-35

—◆━◆━◆—

If you always pay your bills late, your blessings are likely to be on hold.

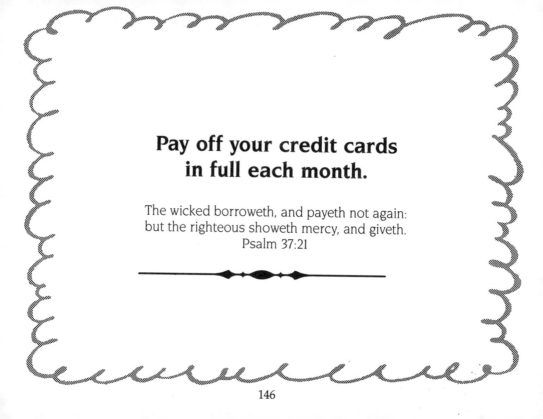

Pay off your credit cards
in full each month.

The wicked borroweth, and payeth not again:
but the righteous showeth mercy, and giveth.
Psalm 37:21

You are in financial trouble if the doorbell, the ringing of the telephone, and the mail cause you to tremble.

If you are borrowing from Peter to pay Paul, remember that Peter has a knife!

Do not trust in riches.

Wilt thou set thine eyes upon that which is not? for riches certainly make themselves wings; they fly away as an eagle toward heaven. Proverbs 23:5

Unload your ship if it is full of debt.

Usually, when there is financial
tension in the home, someone
hasn't been paying attention.

Don't become discouraged by those who have no courage to be flexible.

And I say unto you, Make to yourselves friends of the mammon of unrighteousness; that, when ye fail, they may receive you into everlasting habitations.
Luke 16:9

Most people worry about the end
of the month more than they
worry about the end of the world.

Money can be your master
or your servant.

You will never be without a job if you are the first to help out when something extra needs to be done.

And whatsoever ye do, do it heartily,
as to the Lord, and not unto men.
Colossians 3:23

A lack of discipline will
empty your pockets.

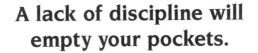

Borrowing should only be considered for
things, such as a home or an education,
that will bring a good return.

The cycle of insufficiency can be broken by the God of all sufficiency.

But my God shall supply all your need according
to his riches in glory by Christ Jesus.
Philippians 4:19

People who can motivate other people will activate a high income for themselves.

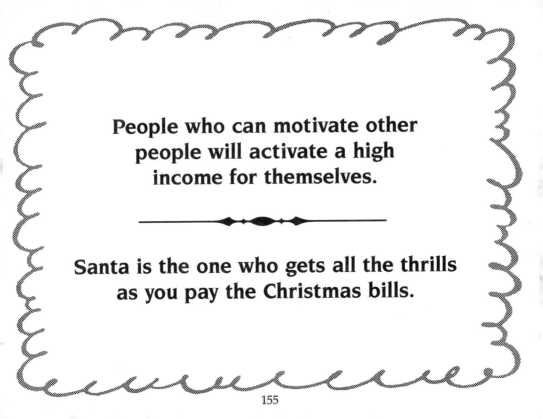

Santa is the one who gets all the thrills as you pay the Christmas bills.

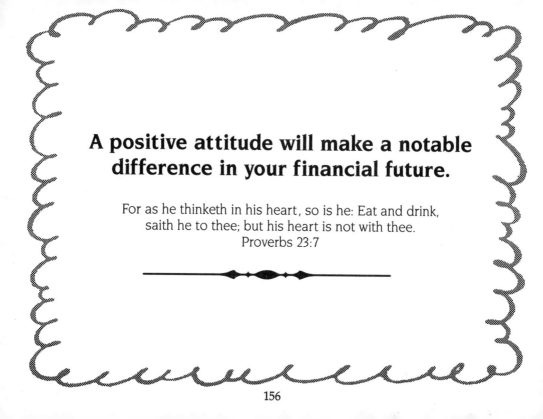

A positive attitude will make a notable difference in your financial future.

For as he thinketh in his heart, so is he: Eat and drink, saith he to thee; but his heart is not with thee.
Proverbs 23:7

About the Authors

Dr. Mack Timberlake, Jr., is pastor of Christian Faith Center in Creedmoor, North Carolina, from where, through diversified methods of television, radio, books, and tapes, the Word of God is launched forth all over the world.

He and his wife, Brenda, minister uniquely together to couples in seminars and by way of their national television program which is seen daily on several national networks.

To contact the authors, write:

Mack and Brenda Timberlake
Christian Faith Center
101 S. Peachtree Street
P. O. Box 100
Creedmoor, NC 27522

Tel.: 919-528-1581
Fax: 919-528-3816